A Purse of Shadows

Heather Newcombe

SUMMER PALACE PRESS

First published in 2010 by

Summer Palace Press

Cladnageeragh, Kilbeg, Kilcar, County Donegal, Ireland
and
31 Stranmillis Park, Belfast BT9 5AU

LOTTERY FUNDED

Printed by Nicholson & Bass Ltd.

A catalogue record for this book is available from the British Library

ISBN 978-1-905989-61-4

FSC

Mixed Sources
Product group from well-managed
forests, controlled sources and
recycled wood or fibre
Cert no. SGS-COC-005221
www.fsc.org
© 1996 Forest Stewardship Council

This book is printed on elemental chlorine-free paper

for Timothy

Acknowledgments

Some of the poems in this book have previously appeared in: *Ulla's Nib*, *The Yellow Nib*, *Myslexia*, *Alchemy* (Creative Writers' Network, 2000) and *In Sight of Rathlin*.

I wish to acknowledge with gratitude the writers Bridget Winter, Geraldine Hawks, Ita McMichael and Anne McCormick, who are no longer with us.

Biographical Note

Heather Newcombe was educated in Coleraine, and now lives in Ballycastle, County Antrim. She is a member of the Ballycastle Writers' Group and has read her work at venues throughout Ireland, including: Poetry Ireland, Dublin; Force 12, Belmullet, County Mayo; Cuirt, Galway; Between the Lines, Belfast; the Wild Geese Festival, Strangford, County Down; Bealtaine Festival, Castlebar, County Mayo and the John Hewitt Spring School, Carnlough, County Antrim.

She was runner-up in the 'Breathing Places Poet-Tree' Competition run by the Western Education and Library Board and the BBC in 2007, and in the Winchester University Poetry Prize 2009.

Her work has been published in magazines in America and Ireland and has been anthologised in *Poetry Now* (1997); *Bear in Mind*, Lagan Press (2000); *Alchemy* (2000); *The Rhythm of Hearts*, Ballycastle Writers' Anthology; *Irish Women Writers* (2006) and *The Sketch, the Ship, and the Afternoon – Ten Years at the Summer Palace* (2009). One poem has been recorded on DVD for Force 12, Belmullet, County Mayo.

A former columnist with the Creative Writers' Network magazine, she tutors creative writing. Her first collection of poetry, *Almost Dancing*, was published by Summer Palace Press in 2004.

CONTENTS

Gas Mask 1959

The summer I was eight
I washed the dust of
generations in the ripple
of a rain barrel,
pressed my face
into the snout,
mouth to mouth with the mask.

I see how it might have been;
shadows crossing the house,
the sun turning the tall stained
glass to coloured mud,
sounds piling high with the drone
of bombers and cries of the dying.

A beat of blood – a small
pulse in my head;
thermal energy floating
outside the perished polymers;
field artillery, a name, a coin,
inked over now by time.

Conversation with J.F.K.

Inaugurated the day I was ten,
he moved a nation to tears.

I remember your picture in
a neighbour's house, you and the Pope,
side by side over the hearth.

Smaller, now that I am taller;
smiling, with blood on his coat.

Sure wasn't pleasant, his voice
rolls around like Californian surf.

When you died I was buying
Senior Service for my mother
in Holly's Shop.
No one said, 'Have a nice day'.

The Vietnam War, he says,
I had it sussed,
and I believed him.

The Summer I Was Eight

unyoked and turned loose
into weather warm as
a pigeon's breast.
The sky-room of my days
big-eyed and blue.
White linen lay across
the hedges.
Flapping lines
of washing whispered in
a foreign tongue.
I journeyed into air,
climbed trees, vaulted gates,
tramped in ditchwater fields,
the summer I was eight,
unyoked and turned loose.

Thinking of Hands

She is thinking of hands
that lie east of the river.
Hands that shook
on a gentlemen's agreement.
Hands that caged the fear
on her first day at school,
that threw the ball gently
so she could catch it.
Made rabbit shadows
on a bedroom wall
to make her laugh
when sick.
Hands that held her
upright on her first bike.
Hands that clapped out
the rhythm of a lost song.
Hands that cupped water
from the well at the end
of the lane.
In summers when it never rained.

Dog on the Moon

I can step towards
the child in the doorway.
A wedge of light
casts her in shadow.
She laps her coat tighter,
her nightdress flutters beneath it.
Cold seeps into her bones.
It is almost Christmas.

Her face is tilted,
she keeps a lone vigil.
A full moon slips
in and out of cloud.
In the black vastness –
a Sputnik and a dog,
whose name is Laika.
It's the only Russian name
she knows.

Her dog Ben is white.
He will get run over.
She will carry him lifeless
from the road, lay him
on a sack,
wait for her father
who will cry as he digs
the grave.
Tonight Ben's safe by the fire.

Laika wide-eyed and scared.
Monitors beep and whirr
on her chest.
Codes tap out on miles
of paper in Moscow.

The child berates the injustice
in her six-year-old heart.
She's not heard of claustrophobia,
but it suffocates her.
She grieves for the 'dog-naut'
who will never come home.
Oxygen exhausted,
spinning weightless in space.

The Lesson

I came upon her,
a rooster held in the well
of her skirt,
the head snapping off in her hand.
The limp cockscomb scarlet
as pomegranate seed.

He staggered in circles,
a drunken headless dance,
stripped vertebrae,
bloodied skin folds
hanging in a grotesque cowl.

Pale and plucked he boiled in a pot.
I couldn't look at him.
His fabulous feathers in a pile
behind the barn.

The Legacy

She left me
a fake diamond ring
sharp-eyed as herself; it cannot be
forced on my index finger
even with soap.

She left me
the memory of two-shilling pieces,
half crowns, brass thrupenny bits.

She left me
the extravagant pleasure of so much money.

She left me
a sense of importance,
her need of me – her childlessness.

She left me
the smell like cordite, metallic sparks
on wire, the thud of bumper cars.

She left me
the taste of ice cream and salty bottomless water.

She left me independence;
the first woman in our family to drive a car.

She left me
disappointed when she wrote on my wedding gift,
'To Heather'.

She left me regret,
the wasted years she'd banished me, *her favourite.*

She left me silent,
ancestral voices drowning mine.

She left me
standing outside the hospital
wanting to see her
before she died –
her belief that Catholics
ate their children
stopping me in my tracks.

An Unholy Ritual

She made a damask
of the torn rags,
frayed them
in a loose lattice
across the table –
a penniless offering
on scrubbed wood.
She sectioned my hair,
tightened it in
tourniquets –
over and under,
over, under …
Fat white sausages
of cloth hung
on my shoulders;
a deserted carousel
of swinging ropes.
Twisted
her own short hair
into pipe cleaners.
It stood on end
in shocked
woollen spikes.
She layered her face
with *Ponds* cold cream,
dotted my nose
in a snowy peak.
Woodland Lavender
or *Woolworths* Body Mist.

Wedged pink mules
wobbled silently
on dark stairs.

Dented dreams
bedded down.
Our crown of thorns
ached dully into the night.

No Ordinary Woman

On Saturday nights
she prepared
the Sunday dinner
and strawberry jelly
in a bowl; the red
squares clear as glass
growing smaller and
smaller in the swirl
of steamy water.
He, leaning in the doorway
watching her,
the smell of night on him.
The wooden spoon
scarlet as sin in her hand.

Rain on Ice

in memory of Stephen

A patch of ice,
a tree, its branches held
outward to the light.

Under a sheet
that held no reason,
past language
that made sense.

The shadow of a bruise
on his left cheek
red as the sky over Orra.

Screams stick in her throat.
Air is rationed.

His chair is empty
at the table.
She lets him go day by day –
a future unlived,
an unbearable silence.

When he was ten,
carving his name on the doorstep.
Now water lies in the broad downstrokes,
green with winter algae.

She touches the cut concrete,
traces the name with her fingers.
The surface is rough,
ridged as a badly healed scar.

The Gamekeeper's Gun

At night he cleaned it,
checked it, broke the barrel.
It lay like a metal wing
across his knee.

How he shot his wife
he never knew.
The master stood for him,
saved him from the gallows.

At ten his eldest balanced
on a chair baking bread
to feed their need, their
starving endless hunger.

His children scattered to the four winds.
Too many to feed, to clothe,
to put things right.
Motherless babies crying in the night.

The man who saved his neck
shared the same surname.
It was never explained.
More blood than water ran through their veins.

At Roonavoolin

for Liam

Sir Roger Casement's body is buried in Dublin
under several tonnes of concrete to prevent his last
wish being granted. Murlough Bay in his beloved
Glens of Antrim was his chosen place of burial.

If the notion took it
to slip into the water,
drift quietly with the tide,
it wouldn't surprise me,
this wood-decked cottage
loosely rigged,
ready as a schooner,
roof hips anchored
into rock and clay.

Cows curious as children
stare at us
through wide windows.
Seabirds fly low,
wings heavy
with summer rain.

Behind the dry stone wall
seed grass turns pink.
In a wet corner
wild iris past its best.
At Smugglers' Cove
the Customs House
is a toothless ruin;
its deserted wall-stead
basalt black.

Seal tongues roll out
the wail of the banshee.
Beyond Fairhead,
Murlough Bay
lies hidden.
In its stony soil
an undug grave.

Snow on His Boots

in memory of Malachy McGurran

All of them smoke roll-ups,
drink from cans – I do neither.
He is white South African.
He says he loves me,
this long-haired activist
plotting revolution.
Marx, he says and *Mao,*
Lenin, Trotsky, Stalin,
names that sound like
liquorice.
I'm not sure of them,
their doctrines
strange, obscure.

Leon Trotsky was
stabbed in the head
with an ice-pick.
He bit the assassin's hand.
Two hundred thousand mourners
in Mexico City for his funeral.
It's not much to go on –
but it's a start.

Trotsky was Stalin
in embryo, a prose stylist,
a polemicist – but a jargonist.
I turn this on my tongue.
There's no such word as jargonist I tell him.
I think I have something on him.

Gestetnered pamphlets
flip to the floor a little blurred,
my fingers black with ink.
I'm good at this.
I can make glue
from flour and water;
hang upside down to paste
posters on a bridge;
smuggle literature;
shout *S.S.R.U.C.*
until my lungs might burst.

Quick at running from
the water cannon's purple blast;
throwing stones.
I am the banner painter,
the slogan writer.

Petit bourgeois, communist,
anarchist, atheist, fundamentalist,
Bolshevik,
I'm on an unknown roll
far from the mission hall.

Revolutionary rhetoric
we risk our necks for,
storm the Winter Palace.
In Derry we relive the October Revolution;
a straggle of battered marchers
wet and weary,
hemmed into Duke Street.

Anniversary 1972
for Cathal

The bare hedges, barbed
as rolls of wire, kennel
you like a dog.

With a blunt Stanley blade
you carve for me
entwined hearts
from the harsh nerves of old wood,
press them into my hand
as I leave
imprinting their shape
on this, our fourth anniversary.
An ancillary happiness.

Later I write abstract
narratives; only one battered
indecipherable stanza still
remains – the currency of survival.

At the Cenotaph

At the Hong Kong cenotaph
we lay a wreath,
each to our own Irish dead
in Crossmaglen and elsewhere.
Unspoken names hang
in the smoggy sunshine,
memories combusting in our chests.

Here where they strutted their colonial might
I think of Joe McCann, the war not yet begun –
shot down in the Markets,
of Hatchet Kerr, Billy McMillan and
too many others.
Of Queen Victoria dipping
shamrock in ink to make it blue.

The Hong Kong club across the square
welcomes us '*even without a tie*'
to its opulent interior; its shameful history
hidden behind oak-panelled walls.
A woman whose great-grandmother was from Tipperary
grows shamrock in her garden;
tells us she ate it once, her North African house boy
mixing it in stew.
She talks in a clipped English accent
of James Joyce and Oscar Wilde.
I am glad I will be going home.

Poet in Pursuit of Silence

She is writing.
He is drowning in the silence.
Endless trips along the hall
closing doors.
The house fills up with noise.

His voice drifts below the door.
Bits of songs – mumbo jumbo.
When she thinks it's over
he excels himself with
a burst of table drumming.

She is distraught.
Words she'd caught and held
slip away from her.
He talks to the dog.
Thankful it can't answer back,
she is filled with dark thoughts of murder;
dark words stab themselves onto the page.

New Shoes

When life is cold,
I pull on winter boots
snug at the ankle.
Well soled,
dependable and sure.

When life breaks up
I don't want new shoes.
Not Stella McCartney
or Jimmy Choo.
Elastoplasts on skin
rubbed raw
just doesn't do it.

Bloodied heels
in white school socks.
It's something you never
forget.

New shoes will always
let you down.

First Impressions

We're in the Milk Bar
when he drops it
casually
into the conversation.
Lincoln appears to him
some nights
standing at the bottom
of his bed, staring.

Abraham?, I say.
*Did the bullet leave
a hole in his cheek?
Did you ask what he'd
thought of the show...
how he felt when
the gun pressed
behind his ear?*

*The man was a
drama himself
taking nine hours to die.
His saintly image –
Shirley Temple
curled up on his lap.*

Did you know
he may have had
Marfan syndrome,
being nine inches taller
than the average man?
The brute
infected his wife;
it's recorded
she had 'presidentially'
acquired third-stage syphilis.
'General paralysis of the insane'.
Thought herself destitute,
sewed money and bonds
into her underwear.

He is silenced.

Beloved

It's difficult.
Stone, cold, dismal…
summing up a life
on a slab of stone.
They would have to
look at it forever.
Carefully chosen words.

Obvious options,
empty adjectives;
Beloved, I suggest.
The thin lips barely move.
John, she says,
*just **JOHN.***

A Purse of Shadows

The onions that year grew full,
their firm breasts swollen out of the soil.
She laid them in rows to dry in the sun,
their shocked roots still gripping the earth.
In the kitchen she wove them into a rope –
strung them from a beam.
In the Rembrandt dimness their green
shoots turned yellow, dry as straw.
The smell of them gathered in her throat,
made her think of him, the onion seller
from Orlean.
She wanted him to lay his plum beret
on the table and dance with her,
a fertility dance organic with tenderness.
She never unstrung the plait or cut them free;
in time their fullness withered to empty husks,
each silver ring a shrunken promise.

First Visit Home
for Megan

Nasturtiums remind me of you:
crimsons, orange-yellows.
Our first grandchild, Irish
in England. You were two
when you first came into
the stillness of our lives
and made yourself at home.

When they called you to leave
you hid among the nasturtiums.

Dance Teacher

for Catriona

In Sai Kung harbour
water taxis thrub the water,
their clinker-built bodies squat
as brown thumbs.

Feathery refugees from China's winter
casually float on the thermals
in search of food.

The islands lie close to land,
link hands as if
they have been dropped there
by accident
to wait for the music.
The sea whispers their birth names.

The girl sees it all from her window,
her face translucent
as a daylight moon.
Her life suspended
between two worlds.
She wonders how to begin again.

A Dead Cat Sings

for Aislinn

The music teacher
gives her a cello.
She is six –
it's bigger than her
and won't fit in the car boot.

She draws the bow
across its throat,
an alley cat opens its
pink-roofed mouth
in full yowl,
its gut squeezed
to the highest pitch.

Each night her eyes
follow the dog-eared
sheets that flop to the floor.
We are in this together:
screaming horsehair
and catgut.

For half a year
the sound is dragged
from a crater torn open.
Her small knees tighten
and loosen around its wide hips.
It wails and groans
between them.

Half notes glitter in the dark.
Soft vibrations slide above
the bending bridge –
resin-dusted and steady.
Her face shines;
the hollow belly resounds
to her allegro strokes.
She has moulded the sound
into music.

A Boy in Red Pyjamas
for Shorna

Your cries split open the night.
We stumbled over ourselves
into nowhere.

Your grandfather
shook loose the newel post;
the stairs shuddered
with his grief.

Your father
sat apart from comfort.
In the scalding silence
seeing your small arms
folded in sleep,
before he laid you down;
before the boiling water
seeped through;
before it welded metal studs
into your small leg;
before your wails of agony
filled his head;
before the ambulance arrived.

Your mother,
collapsing inside herself,
believed she had lost you.
At ten days old,
you clung in agony to life.

We sent for Pat, who had *the gift*.
You laid your tiny hand on his.

I
knew then you would survive,
knew with certainty you *would* walk.

Angels Eat Pizza
for Tiarnan

I am reading him a story.
He cuddles on my knee –
he is three, tells me he is
frightened of dogs and the dark.
I tell him he is safe,
a guardian angel
sits on his shoulder.
He touches each shoulder
and smiles, knows it's
part of the story.
Eating pizza for tea
he earnestly turn-takes,
lifting
each slice to his shoulder,
feeds the angel:
a bite for you
and a bite for me.

Visiting

He had seen them all off.
Important people, he says,
die young. I
can't get away.

He talks as if going on a trip.
Today his glass is half empty;
we are reduced to talk of porridge.
It gets him through the night,
the smell of cream and syrup.

He had a hard life;
has condensed the bad times
into a litany
he can recite by heart:
freezing cold mornings; six miles
on a bicycle; long hours and bad pay.

I struggle to pull him back,
draw him to his greenhouse
that once bulged with fat tomatoes,
leeks thick as a man's arm,
the black hyacinth grafted to beetroot
to baffle the neighbour.

Do you mind the time?, he says,
and I do.
Ordinary things
that were extraordinary
in their ordinariness.

I drive into the night,
remember him sitting on my bed
when I was a child –
will he think of this, I wonder,
between yawns, waiting for
morning and the smell
of porridge?

Stoat Song

Was it only last week
you came to my door,
your damp nose pressed
against the bright glass
and your reflection?
Did you find me out of fear
or desperation,
frantic to find your other self
wildly weaving back and forth?
Mesmerised, I let you in, watched
your fruitless darting and diving,
the pungent smell of you.

I willed you to leave,
return to the ditches and fields.
I begged you to give up the search;
you would not go.
I trapped you in a black net.
You lay limp and smouldering,
snared in its spidery folds –
sent out your appalling scent.
I put you in a birdless aviary,
named you *Galileo.*
I strung up a linen hammock
like those I saw for polecats
in *Les Ramblas,* Barcelona.
Fed you raw mince, bone and hair
stuck on a long skewer.
I was repulsed and excited.

Each day you descend
from your lofty bed –
a ball of indignant hunger –
bark a warning before you feed.
I am warm with the proximity
of your presence, that you trust
me – even a little.

One day you will leave.
I know there will be
no fond farewell.

Pools of Light

for my mother

She lies awake,
her curtains drawn
against an August dawn.
Today will be
like yesterday.
The house less clean,
the rainbows more
mysterious.
The pools of light
without edge or boundary.

She's lived the fear for years.
A story in Braille,
the lives of fishermen
long dead in oily wool.
The 'tock tock' of her
Grandmother's cane
striking the floor.
The click wooden beads
make on string.

Market in Provence

At the *brocante*
we buy
a Box Brownie.

In the worn leather case
a roll of film:
sepia figures
from before the war;
bathing booths on hot sand;
an ice bucket,
its tarnished silver
lustreless and dull –
trapped in its emptiness
echoes of clinking flutes,
burgundy boudoirs,
pink-washed chalets,
the smiles of
whores and harlots.

Also, a solid brass stamp –
heavy with importance
it rests in my hand,
an imprint of acceptance
or privilege.
I will take it home,
make of it a souvenir,
let dust settle on its
authority.

Time for Home
for unknown woman with cow

She rounded the corner,
a juggernaut of flesh
broad and round as her cow,
a hank of worn rope drooped across
its horns; a lopsided bovine halo of hemp.
She holds the cow to heel, like a terrier.
Her eyes shine bright as headlamps.
The cow's cow eyes, submissive and wet,
coolly observe us.

We are too shocked to greet them.
How does one address a woman and
her cow in Turkish?
They are as brown as each other,
as steadfast in their purpose,
their feet already in a greener place.

Evening traffic streams out behind
her – she holds the centre of the road:
a woman and a cow taking their place.

No one dares overtake her.
Reverently they hold their distance,
wearily wait; in Gundogan
respect is shown to women and their cows.

At the Feet of Pasternak

These days I come to the dacha –
he's not good at walking.

Zina shows me in,
she has a basin ready.
I draw off the coarse grey socks,
wrap one foot in red felt
I've brought in my basket,
lay the other naked on my knee,
coat the papery skin with oil,
massage the swollen ankle,
feel the flat patterned stress
of his sole push against my hand.

Zina is watching.
Oh what feet the poet
walks upon, what bunions, bumps
and bent toes, she mocks.

When she leaves, he tells me
she used to suck his toes.
I am afraid she is listening
and will rush in yelling abuse,
accuse me of anything
that comes into her crazy head.

Yesterday she threatened
to throw herself under a train.

He is bent with regret,
soft-boned idioms
and metres of missed chances.
A rub, a potion for all I lost,
he demands of me.

How can I tell him I'm lost myself
and a little in love with Zhivago?

Purple Hearts

for all victims of Agent Orange

I picked it
in the Vietnam jungle,
carried it home
in a toothbrush
holder.
Concealed it
like a drug
I might be
careful to hide.
A live reminder
of my journey,
to grow
in my kitchen.

Jungle inch plant
purple as a scar;
inching its way
through trees,
grounded planes,
crashed helicopters,
rusting tanks.
The remnants
of defeat.
Reminder
of victory.

Amethysts and Sea Gods
for Cahal Óg

A long summer full of rain.
In a ripple of rushes
the bleached shadow of a swan.
On the wet road our footsteps
make a sound like falling stones.

Behind the rough-masoned
walls of the hillside graveyard,
the tomb of generations.
Arum lilies grow tall and white
as hunger.

On Achill, you can almost
walk across the lake. Our
boat hit a telegraph pole.
Where else but Ireland would they
put a pole in the middle of a lake?

The landlord of the dark cavernous
house is a horror writer. A couple
like ourselves sit sheltering from the rain
saying they should have gone to Spain.

At the west end of the island, I find
an amethyst seam scored across the stone,
its cool weathered touch rough,
sharp as bone.

In a flash of purple light
Manannan McLir rises
from the water, the crown
of Aphrodite in his teeth.

When I Want to Die I Sew Instead

Stitch by stitch I pin anger in.
Great loops of tangled thread
jam the shuttle race.
I am over-locking burnished golds,
blazing crimsons, deep sultry
river browns; monogramming
the web and weave.

No pasty pastels belie
the pain in each blind hem.
I remember every row,
grieve for all that was left unspoken.
A washed-out thickness
drains all that is simmering
into the unsuspecting fabric,
as I appliqué out the shell-tucked
memories of past betrayals,
slipstitching them into a small
square patch of scarlet silk.

Fear of the dark

By my gate
the banshee waits
leafless and lurking.
Deep eye sockets,
a grey peaked hood
hugging the dark.

I am turning into
my mother.
My irreverent
fear irrational.
An unwanted baton
pressed into
my hand,
I will not pass on.

Shadows on the wall

My father's hands
made animal shadows
on the wall.
Softened the edges
and corners of childhood
dreams.

Now my silent shadow,
neither tactile
nor breathing, stretches
across rough-masoned
gateposts;
lies flat against
the piled-up sky;
the oddly slanting light
driven out by the dark
wedge of night.

Testament

She wrapped me
in winceyette
'combinations'
from Miss Luke's
on Main Street;
swaddled me
in liberty bodices and
sensible interlock knickers.
Herself
in salmon coloured stays
boned, to hold her in –
a woman
who caught her breath.
She bought me coats with
velveteen collars.
Took me to Gospel meetings
on Sunday nights
where men gave testaments
and ruddy-faced farmers cried.

Sleeping with Geraniums

Geraniums in china pots
watch over the fields.
Season after season old roots give up
the same ragged leaf;
cane, split with age, deep
in the shrunken soil.
Pot-bound roots, translucent white,
sightless as spiders' eggs.
Pink petals pale as early loss
staining the window sill.
Knuckled limbs the colour of old flesh
trapped in the gap between net and glass.

Ashes to Ashes

Years later I am thinking of her
in a black coat – *the cut of her* –
it half shut, flapping
like a drift of wings.
The salt-and-pepper crown of her
head bobbing and the slap
of shoes against her heel.

A woman, regal in a black hat,
who drove a hearse because she had to;
closed the eyes of the dead;
drank tea that tarred up cup and tongue;
knew a thing or two about hard times.

After her death I missed her on the street.

She was the bullet in a gun that stuck.
The newest butterfly, white and green.
A broken pot, a bright new glass of water.
A silver piece that could have been the moon.

Townlands of Torr

for Siobhan and Marie in memory of Anne

On the journey to your own place
I marked out the townlands of Torr.
Past *Doey's Planting* the small burn,
slate grey and silver.

At Ballyukin School
snowdrops hid under hedges.
Up Merrick's Brae,
at Ballyloghan, we stopped
outside your house,
climbed the Green Hill.

The Mull and
Spoon Island watched our passing
over *Mary Lynn's Bridge.*

We lowered you into the cool *Coolraney* clay,
pressed you into sleep with heavy hearts.
Your girls stoic and strong, your grandsons,
small figures in black, stood
in the weak sunshine shaking hands,
their faces wept of colour.

Adrian

for Jackie

When you died big men cried.
The town was shocked
to tears.
Shops closed;
staff stood silent.

I imagined
you'd have smiled,
not quite believing.

The sea in your blood,
you'd face a 'force nine'
to keep a promise,
ride the churning channel
between here and Rathlin.

You're much too alive
to be dead.

In Sight of a New Space
for Micky

I have created
in his absence
a place light and hopeful.
Three days of dust,
broken bricks, have given way
to open space.
In the window, the sea
through stark sycamores.

The workmen were nervous,
not sure of me,
asking, 'What'll he say?'
He knows, I said,
I'm up to something.
I'm not sure they believed me.
They were a biddable crowd.
A friend who was in on the secret
e-mailed; R.T.E. were sending a crew.
We were high as kites.

When he returned – there were pink
hydrangea and wine on a table
so big we could play snooker.
To fit our brood and their brood;
all of us around it –
all touching the same wood.
He was relieved he said,
he thought
I'd be raising the roof.